EUCHARISTIC MINISTERS

Brian Glennon

Eucharistic Ministers

A HANDBOOK

the columba press

First published in 2012 by
the columba press
55a Spruce Avenue, Stillorgan Industrial Park,
Blackrock, Co Dublin

Designed by Bill Bolger
Origination by The Columba Press
Printed in Ireland by
Turners Printing Company Ltd, Longford

ISBN 978 1 85607 766 8

Contents

Foreword

The Eucharist is at the heart of Christian community. In celebrating the Eucharist, the community recalls how it came into existence, namely through the total self-giving of its founder and leader, the Risen Jesus, whose body was broken and whose blood was poured out for the sake of his brothers and sisters. The community then listens to the command of Jesus: 'Do this in memory of me', and goes out with a deepened commitment to follow on that same path of radical self-giving. The community, therefore, brings to the Eucharist the cares, concerns and needs of the community; and the community leaves the Eucharist with a firm commitment to reaching out to meet those needs, no matter the cost.

As the pagans observed the early Christian communities, what astounded them was not so much their prayer life, or their beliefs, but their extraordinary love for one another: 'See how they love one another', they said to each other in amazement. Each member of the community therefore has a ministry to love, to care and to share, a ministry of radical solidarity with each other and radical acceptance of those who, in the wider society, feel rejected and unwanted. Participation in the Eucharist, then, is not for those who want a quiet life or those who do not want to leave their comfort zones. In the Eucharist, we celebrate the love story which is the life, death and resurrection of Jesus, and we commit ourselves to continuing that story in the chapter of our own lives and of our own self-sacrifice.

These reflections for those considering becoming ministers of the Eucharist present both a challenge and an invitation. The challenge is to live what they do: as they distribute the Body of Christ to their community in the church building, they are called also to share themselves with the Body of Christ which is the community. Those who minister at the Eucharist must be a model to their community of self-giving, in imitation of the One at whose altar they serve.

The invitation is to enter into the fullness of joy which is the fruit of love, kindness and compassion. As we open our hearts to include others in our love, we grow more fully human and, therefore, more into the image and likeness of God. It is an invitation to make that leap of faith which defies reason, to discover the fullness of joy that comes from bringing joy to others.

While this book was written as preparatory reflections for ministers of the Eucharist, it will be of immense value to all who wish to deepen their understanding of the Eucharist, and who wish to participate more fully in the Eucharist.

Peter McVerry SJ

Preface

It was a great pleasure and honour to be a tutor for over twenty years to those training as Eucharistic Ministers in the Dublin diocese. I would like to thank the many students who participated in the courses for their commitment and sincerity as they faced a new challenge in their lives. These reflections are dedicated to them.

I would like to thank my theology teacher, Fr Enda Lyons DD, who in my younger years fired me with enthusiasm for theology and related topics and has been a good friend ever since. His 'firing' has kept me going and this book is one result of it.

I am delighted to offer any royalties that will accrue from the sale of the book to the Peter McVerry Trust. The trust works in the area of homelessness and addiction. As you read this book, I hope you will begin to connect this kind of working for justice with what it means to celebrate the Eucharist.

I welcome your comments at brianglennon@eircom.net

Introductory Reflections

1 DEAR READER

Thank you for taking the time to use this little book of reflections for Eucharistic Ministers. The reflections grew out of my experience of tutoring those on preparation courses for this ministry in the Dublin diocese for over twenty years. They are based on my teaching and notes; however, in this book format I do not have the wonderful facility I had to open the teaching in a dialogue fashion, the cut and thrust of the 'live' classroom, the participants seeking clarification and elaboration, and of course adding their own experiences and wisdom.

I would encourage you to use this little book almost entirely as an aid to quiet, reflective time. It is by no means an academic handbook. It is quite simply a series of reflections for those involved in Eucharistic Ministry – either considering the ministry or preparing for it. For those already ministering for some time it might help as a quiet pause, a time to look at how you are ministering. The most important part of these reflections may well be your time spent on considering and mulling over the questions found after each reflection.

I have tried to link ministry and life, liturgy and life throughout the reflections. This comes from my belief that who you are as a person will colour the quality and reverence of your ministry. It is not about a 'performance' at the celebration of the

Eucharist, unhinged from the rest of your life. Your life can nourish and bless your ministry and, of course, your ministry can nourish and bless your life. As I quote later from Richard Rohr: 'How we do anything is how we do everything.'

Your ministry ought to become part of your life's journey. Life's journey may be experienced as a call to integrity; a call to love and to live for what is good and true. In the prayer after communion you pray: 'What has passed our lips as food, Lord, may we possess in purity of heart.' It is this 'purity of heart' that opens you up to God's presence in your life and to a generous response. Unfortunately in today's world integrity and purity of heart may be absent in our leaders, in church and state. This is all the more reason for you to nurture your ministry with prayerful reflection.

As 'the love of God has been poured into our hearts by the Holy Spirit, who has been given to us,' let us respond generously. Responding to this is building what has traditionally been called the kingdom of God or, more inclusively, the reign of God. The following quote is one way of elaborating on this:

> Wherever the human heart is healed, justice gains a foothold, peace holds sway, an ecological habitat is protected, wherever liberation, hope and healing break through, wherever an act of simple kindness is done, a cup of cool water given, a book offered to a child thirsty for learning, there the human and earth community already reflect, in fragments, the visage of the Trinitarian God. Borne by 'the grace of our Lord Jesus Christ, the love of

God, and the fellowship of the Holy Spirit', we become committed to a fruitful future inclusive of all peoples, tribes, and nations, all creatures of the earth. The reign of God gains another foothold in history' (Johnson, p 224).

May your reflective time be blessed richly and your life and ministry reflect that blessing.

2 *'THE FULLNESS OF JOY IS TO BEHOLD GOD IN EVERYTHING.'*
(Julian of Norwich)

This is the challenge of our Christianity; the invitation to see, recognise and respond to the inherent sacredness that approaches us in our lives, in our communities, in our living and loving, in our doing justice each day. We must remember of course that it is an 'approach' that is inherent in our being human, not the preserve of religions or churches. God approaches people in unconditional love, loving kindness and compassion. That becomes the example for us to follow.

Eucharistic ministry belongs in this context and must remain rooted there to be genuine. It is this mystery of the sacred incarnated that is celebrated in the Eucharist; the mystery that I myself am. Augustine says:

> If, then, you want to understand the Body of Christ, remember what the apostle says: 'You are the Body of Christ and member thereof' (1Cor 12:27). If, then, you are the Body of Christ and his member, it is your mystery which is set forth on the Lord's table; it is your own mystery that you receive. You say 'Amen' to what you are and in saying 'Amen' you subscribe to it. For you hear the words: 'The Body of Christ' and you answer 'Amen'. Be members of the Body of Christ, then, so that your 'Amen' might be authentic.

The authenticity of your 'Amen' and of your Eucharistic ministry will be closely related to your ability to behold God in everything and allow that become the fullness of joy for you. It is in the integration of your understanding and response to the 'God in everything' and your understanding and response to being the 'Body of Christ' that will authenticate and inspire your Eucharistic ministry just as it authenticates and inspires your baptism and your humanity.

This may sound rather heavy for you as reader. The 'Body of Christ' means how we unite ourselves with the work and mission of Jesus – to bring about a world where love, peace, joy, compassion and justice are the order of the day. In your commitment to this work you become the 'Body of Christ' – responding to God's call in everything you do, think and say.

If you are a minister of the Eucharist or considering or preparing for that ministry, then what I have said above becomes part of your prayer and part of your living; you cannot minister the fullness of joy without it being in some way the air you breathe. My experience of tutoring courses over many years has let me in on a big secret – so many of the wonderful people I have had the privilege to work with have this fullness of joy in beholding God in everything, but somehow needed it to be recognised and affirmed for them and then knitted into their understanding and experience of being the 'Body of Christ'.

Take time out silently to allow the words: 'The fullness of joy is to behold God in everything,' to percolate into your mind and heart. What might the consequences of this be for you?

3 THE 'HOLY MYSTERY' IN YOU

How do you experience God ... is it down to you or
up to God? How do you fit God into your world or
is that question more correctly put the other way
round?

> We cannot discover God directly or indirectly as we
> might find a subatomic particle in the trailings of a
> cloud chamber. God is not one being who appears
> alongside other beings that exist, not even if we
> envision God as the greatest one, or the first, or the
> last. It is a mistake to think of God as an element
> within a larger world, or as part of the whole of real-
> ity. Holy mystery cannot be situated within our sys-
> tem of co-ordinates but escapes all categories.
> Hence, to think rightly of God we must give up the
> drive to intellectual mastery and open up to the
> Whither of our spirit's hungry orientation. 'The con-
> cept God is not a grasp of God by which a person
> masters the mystery; but it is the means by which
> one lets oneself be grasped by the mystery which is
> ever present yet ever distant' (Johnson, p 36).

As we grow spiritually we become more comfortable with allowing ourselves to 'be grasped' by
God and realise that this is what the fullness of joy
is and what the 'Body of Christ' is inviting us to
experience. Have you ever sensed being grasped by
God? How did it feel? Perhaps it was being blown
away by a sunset or a piece of music? Maybe it was
when you first laid eyes on your daughter/son and
held her/him close? Or when you fell in love, your
first kiss? Perhaps it is an experience you have each
day: as you jump out of bed, greet a new day, pause
for a 'now' moment in the midst of a busy schedule,

share a tear with someone who needs you at that moment or spend a quiet moment of thanks at the end of the day?

As we explore our innermost sacred selves 'we run into God'. This is really good news – we need never be afraid. It is the 'letting go and letting God'; something familiar to those whose life journey is accompanied by an addiction of one kind or other. 'Letting go and letting God' helps us on the road to recovery, welcoming being 'grasped by God' rather than being convinced that I can do it alone. One way for this to happen is to slow down:

> Of course our hyperactivity can keep us adrift on the surfaces of ourselves and unable to reach deeper levels of desire. So we need to prepare the way of the Lord, as the gospel says, through attending to our own mystery first. It is never just our own mystery: it is the place where God pitches a tent in our deepest self ... Here our spirit can blossom into wonder before the mystery of ourselves ... Through such human openings we glimpse the greater mystery of God's self-giving to us in Christ. When we take time to pause and listen to our hearts, in the surprise of silence we find ourselves encountering more than the mystery of our small life. We experience our desire for something more than outer living. I would say that here, so to speak, we run into God and can become in a sense everyday mystics (Gallagher, pp 47-48).

Open your heart in silence and allow yourself to be grasped by the Holy Mystery ... pray for this grace. This is the invitation you extend as a Eucharistic Minister, facilitating the 'running into God'.

4 *SUNDAY EUCHARIST: WHY GO?*

In his book, *Liturgy Made Simple*, Mark Searle poses the question as to why people attend Mass. Is it because they like a particular parish, or they are obliged to attend, or because they find some meaning in it? He suggests that going to the celebration of the Eucharist is a response to an invitation – God calling us together. The initiative is God's and the response is ours. Nowadays we see people engaged on Sundays in a broad variety of activities and this means that going to church becomes a very definite choice. This choice is part of our lifestyle, in choosing to find meaning and nurture in religion, spirituality, Christianity. In going to church on Sundays we commit ourselves to seeking and responding to the call to be the kingdom of God: 'to act justly, love tenderly and walk humbly with your God' (Micah 6:8).

> Thus the coming together of the congregation is a sign and symbol of what God is doing and where his work is going. God's work in history … is to gather into one the scattered children of God, to overcome divisions, to provide a place for the homeless and the lonely, to give support to those whose burdens are heavy, and to create an oasis of community in the midst of a world painfully divided into the haves and the have-nots. Here, in the congregation of God, we are all to discover our common humanity and to set aside our inequities. The gathering of believers is meant to be the anticipation of the day when God's kingdom will be established in all its fullness, when there will be no more discrimination on the grounds of sex, race or

wealth; when there will be no more hunger and thirst, no more mistrust and mutual violence, no more competitiveness and abuse of power, for all things will be subject to Christ and God will reign over his people in peace and for ever (Searle, pp 212-22).

Spend some reflective time on the previous paragraph. Is this how you see God's work in history, the coming of God's reign ... what part do you play? The quote above is very aspirational ... does it really happen and how?

5 THE 'HOLY MYSTERY' IN LITURGY AND LIFE: THE REIGN OF GOD

In a well known discourse, St John Chrysostom stressed the close connection between Jesus present on the altar and Jesus present in the poor:

> Do you wish to honour the Body of Christ? Then do not allow it to be scorned in its members, in the poor, who have nothing to clothe themselves with. Do not honour him in church with silk and then neglect him outside when he is cold and naked … What does Christ gain from a sacrificial table full of golden vessels when he then dies of hunger in the persons of the poor? First of all feed the hungry and only then dress the altar with what is left. Would you offer him a golden chalice and refuse him a glass of water? What need is there to dress his altar with gold, if you fail to offer him some necessary clothing? … Therefore while you adorn the place of worship, do not lock your heart to your suffering brother. This is a more precious living temple than the other' (Cantalamessa, p 74).

How does this quotation from St John Chrysostom in the fourth century make you stop and think; think and act? Does it put some context around your ministry?

6 CALLED TO MINISTRY

People arrive at Eucharistic ministry training courses from a variety of standpoints. Some volunteer
and some are asked. Those who volunteer may
have been attracted to the ministry for many years
but felt slow to offer their service, felt unworthy,
unsure how the priest and neighbours might react.
They wondered if they might be judged for being
too young, a woman, separated from a spouse, an
academic, a gay person, a foreigner, a traveller; not
good enough, not involved in the parish or other
local activities. Some people are delighted to be
asked, others slow in their response. The good thing
about a preparatory course is that it gives you time
to consider all the issues that arise in your mind and
in your heart, whether you were asked or you vol-
unteered. Taking time out to consider this ministry,
in quiet and silent prayer is essential. I believe that
in silence we recognise the nearness of God and in
preparing for eucharistic ministry it is crucial to
spend some time in silence. In this silence we
begin to behold God in everything and the fullness
of joy manifests itself. Perhaps you might consider
a few quiet days away in a monastery guesthouse?
This silence gives you a chance to gather your
thoughts and feelings about the ministry and it
gives God a chance to gather you and your
thoughts and feelings to God!

So many people on my courses have expressed
the feeling that they are 'unworthy' of being called
to eucharistic ministry and that it is a big privilege.

I listen and I respect these expressions and ask them what these feelings are saying to them? How are you unworthy and what is the privilege? Have you been the 'Body of Christ' since your baptism? Has Christ called you into his company as a eucharistic community and gifted you with that call? Has Christ gathered you into his fullness of joy, and made you his very own? This is the air you have been given to breathe and it is the gentle challenge to you to witness in your living and in your loving to see the 'God in everything' so that all may be God's very own. This witnessing is your calling; this gives meaning and reality to your baptism and also to your eucharistic ministry. Are you 'unworthy' and is it a 'privilege'?

How do you experience your call to ministry?

7 ARE YOU 'SUITABLE'?

This is both a complex and a simple question to answer. Answers like being committed to your faith and a natural aptitude for the ministry are on the right track. Which question would you prefer to answer: 'Do you believe in God?' or 'Do you live out God?' The second question implies that,

> authentic faith is not simply an affirmation of God's existence but rather an event-encounter which calls us to a transformation of self and of world (Gallagher, p 95).

How do you see this 'event-encounter'? Is there some way you sense it in your life? This commitment to transformation is at the heart of the reign of God, at the heart of your daily living as a Christian and at the heart of the challenge of the Eucharist. It is the challenge you minister to people as you say: 'The Body of Christ.' It is the challenge they respond to with their 'Amen.' How you respond to many of the reflections in this little book may be an indication of whether or not you are called to this ministry.

Of course ministers of the Eucharist are people for whom the Mass and prayer are central in their living out the reign of God. They do not see their ministry as attached to honour or prestige. They are people,

> who are always ready to do a favour, or a service of the most menial kind, who show up at your door to help when a person is sick or when someone has died. Those who are ready to be 'broken for others' in time and in material goods are possible candidates for the ministry of communion (Communion, p 9).

As regards the public nature of the ministry,

> a minister of Communion has to have some degree of
> social grace. We look for people who are hospitable,
> friendly, compassionate and discreet. Discretion is a
> must in this ministry, and parish gossips simply do
> not have the 'natural' qualifications for this ministry.
> (Communion, p 9).

A certain self-assuredness is necessary. Being at
ease with the ocular, verbal and tactile elements of
the ministry is essential. (To appreciate this better
see later reflection *Ocular, Verbal and Tactile Contact*.)
All of these 'suitabilities' can be nurtured by prayer
and practice. Don't be discouraged initially.

Reflect on the question: 'Do you live out God?' and
where does your eucharistic ministry fit in your
answer? How do you nurture your suitability for the
ministry?

8 TWO PERSONAL REFLECTIONS ON WHAT IT MEANS TO BE A MINISTER OF HOLY COMMUNION

From a young age the Mass and Communion meant a lot to me. As a child I was fortunate to have a front seat in the gallery of our old parish church. Every Sunday morning I had a bird's eye view of the altar and I was fascinated to watch the actions of the priest at Mass and listen to his words.

At secondary school one of my teachers once explained that the Mass was very much a participation ceremony – we speak to God in the Confiteor and Gloria. God speaks to us in the Epistle and Gospel. We then offer our gifts to God with Jesus in the Offertory and God gives Himself back to us in Holy Communion. So we must always be co-participants with Jesus as we offer ourselves with Him to the Father.

In the mid-nineties I discovered that I had cancer. I really believe that my complete healing came about through the wonderful power of the Eucharist – 'Only say the word and I shall be healed.'

When I retired from full-time working, I put my name forward for Ministry of the Eucharist, conscious of what a very special ministry this is ... Jesus coming to us in a special way in Holy Communion.

Some of my elderly neighbours who had attended Mass and Holy Communion every Sunday for years now find it more difficult to get to Mass and

Communion. I now bring Holy Communion to three of them. This is a central part of my week and I am inspired by their deep reverence for Holy Communion. They look forward so much to receiving the Lord. It is also a great link with the Christian Community for them. Their appreciation and reverence has strengthened my faith. It truly is a privilege to be Minister of Holy Communion to the parish community at Mass and to my wonderful neighbours at home.

Bríd Brassill

I have been a Minister of Holy Communion now for nearly two years and my initial reaction on being asked was that this would be a good opportunity of giving something back to the parish in a concrete way. A way of actively participating in parish life.

Two years later my views on being a minister have evolved. I feel I now have a greater understanding of the sacrament of the Eucharist with more of a feeling of ownership of the sacrament and my faith in general.

At the moment the Church is under a lot of pressure with various scandals, and I like many other Catholics have been affected by what we have heard. Being a Minister of the Eucharist has helped me to realise that the Church is not just about the priest on the altar but also about all of us as a community and that the goodness and effectiveness of the Church depends on us all.

What it has done is also show me that you have to invest and work at your faith. It isn't something that you can just leave to chance and hope that it will grow. The discipline of being a Minister has helped me to make that effort and made me reflect more on what my faith means to me. It has helped me to realise that my faith is important to me and how I view the world.

My mother and father were involved in the parish while I was growing up and it had a positive effect on me. I hope that my involvement will serve as guidance to my own children and help them to make the right decisions about their own faith.

Michael Harty
Booterstown,
Co. Dublin

9 EUCHARISTIC MINISTERS ARE THE FRUITS OF THE PARISH COMMUNITY

There is a sense in which all ministries are invitations or callings experienced in the heart and this is where we 'run into God'. One way that ministries are nurtured is by the experience of welcome and hospitality in the faith community; this is the ground in which ministries are planted. Here are some questions which indicate the strength of the hospitality of the Sunday assembly at your parish:

- Do we, the members of the assembly, greet and welcome one another?
- Do we have a sense of what's happening in one another's lives, be it joys, difficulties, sickness, grief, worries, confusion, uncertainty or exciting new adventures?
- Are we close enough to know who is not there, including the sick and homebound ... and those who stay away because they feel excluded or unwelcome?
- Are we concerned about what is happening in the world?
- Do we have a 'big heart'?
- How is everyone welcomed and included, the stranger, the outsider, the marginalised, the neglected, and even those whom society rejects?
- Are we as welcoming as Christ was?
- Does our involvement in the action of the Mass inspire participation in the celebration? (Koester, p 43).

How can you add to the hospitality of your Sunday assembly? What would be your motivation?

A Little History

10 THE STORY OF THE MASS

The Mass is a love story, where we are invited intimately to be part of that story. The story began in God's own loving heart, something like the loving heart of a mother or father; a love desiring to reach out in love, to share and lavish that love on another and a love seeking union with the beloved. God's love is the motivation behind what we call the incarnation – that is the story of God becoming; becoming one of us, living and loving, laughing and crying with us, desiring to be one with us. We are invited to allow God walk with us, to respond to God's challenge to build a world where there is no injustice, no discrimination, where we grow in integrity, purity of heart and loving kindness.

We love stories; they speak to us, they interpret our lives, they celebrate life and tradition and they give meaning. Have you heard the story of the elderly African American woman who saw a picture of the dead Jesus in the arms of his mother, in the window of a Religious Information Centre in the US? She went in and asked: 'That Jesus dead in your window?' 'Yes.' 'He done been killed by the badmans?' 'Yes.' 'Done dead and gone forever, that poor Jesus gone and dead forever, huh?' 'No, he rose again on Easter morning.' 'Rose again? You mean he live again? He rise from the dead? He truly, really rise from the dead?' 'Yes, you must

have heard the story of the resurrection before?'
And with a broad smile, her face bubbling with joy,
the old lady said: 'Oh I done heard it before, I guess
I done heard it a million times before – but I just glo-
ries to hear it again!'

'Jesus is risen!' is the essence of that story and it
is the essence of the love story that is the Mass.
Because Jesus is risen, we celebrate in thanksgiving
(meaning of Greek word *eucharist*); his resurrection
is the stage on which the entire drama of God's love
story with us and with all humanity is definitively
unfolded; beginning with creation in Genesis, continuing through to today and into the future.

*What is your favourite story; your favourite Bible story
... and why? Spend some time in reflective quiet.*

11 *A COVENANT: LOVE AND JUSTICE*

We trace the celebration of the Eucharist to the Last
Supper in the upper room, the Cenacle, in
Jerusalem. It was within the tradition of the celebration of the Jewish Passover. A 'last' supper
implies others. Indeed Jesus shared many meals,
dinner parties, not only with his close friends but
also with those in church and state authority. He
even shared meals with people whom those in
church and state authority not only looked down on
but despised and hated. These meals were truly the
stories of an unconditionally loving God in Jesus,
whose compassion, like that of a true mother or
father, knew 'no limits'. They are the consequence
of a belief that, 'The kingdom of God is within you.'
They were meals of an indiscriminate welcome.

So at the Last Supper Jesus gave thanks and at
our eucharistic celebration we give thanks – for
Jesus and his life and love, his passion for justice –
and also for creation and our environment, for our
lives and loves and for the challenges we face daily,
personally, locally and globally. We give thanks for
a God who is truly on our side:

> In the prophetic texts of the Bible, God is a God of
> pathos who feels intensely: loves, cares, is glad,
> gets angry over injustice, urges, prods, forgives, is
> disappointed, gets frustrated, suffers righteous
> indignation, weeps, grieves, promises, pours out
> mercy, rejoices, consoles, wipes away tears, and
> loves some more' (Johnson, p 56).

This is the God in whose image we are challenged

to be. In this challenge we are called by grace to express our love in care for others and our environment, in the creative arts, literature, music, in the economy, technology and even in liturgy.

Those present at the last supper in a sense represented all humankind – before and after them – for at this supper of thanksgiving is celebrated the distillation of infinite compassion, the high point of the drama of God's engagement in love with creation and all its people. Jesus gave the Passover a new meaning, a covenant of love – the holy mystery of God and humankind as it discovers itself oriented toward that Holy Mystery. This covenant/agreement/sacrifice/invitation/reign of God becomes 'visible in history wherever love of neighbour, faithfulness to conscience, courage for resistance to evil, and any other human witness to what is 'more' takes place' (Johnson p 41). It is this covenant that Jesus celebrated at the Last Supper, a covenant hidden in the dawn of creation and in the human heart. It is this covenant that is the story of the Mass. Those present in the Upper Room participated fully in the celebration – listening, singing and sharing but it took a lifetime to understand and knit together the covenant story and its reality in their lives.

Who do you share your table with ... and how is God present?

12 MASS OF THE APOSTLES

The very early Christian community met in the Jewish Temple and synagogues to pray and listen to their scriptures and teachings and later in the day they met in their homes to 'break the bread'. This didn't last too long as their identity around the Risen Lord began to differentiate them from their fellow Jews and caused problems. They began to bring together the reading of the scriptures and the breaking of bread in their homes and this gathering slowly moved to Sunday from Saturday, remembering the resurrection. They met early in the day as Sunday was the first day of the working week.

At this stage those who joined the original group of Jesus' followers believed the Risen Lord was at the centre of their faith. His life, death, resurrection and ascension into glory became the still point in their turning world, the point against which they discerned how to live, love, seek truth, act justly and pray. It was a vibrant community of believers with very simple structures and equally simple liturgies.

These communities grew, developed and spread around the Roman Empire as it was and we have an account of the celebration of the Eucharist in the early part of the second century, attributed to St Justin:

> On that day which is named after the sun, all who are in the towns and in the country gather together for a communal celebration. And then the memoirs of the apostles or the prophets are read, as

long as time permits. After the reader has finished the one presiding gives an address, urgently exhorting his hearers to practise these beautiful teachings in their lives. Then all stand up together and recite prayers. After the prayers are over, as has already been remarked, the bread and wine mixed with water are brought forward, and the president offers up prayers and thanksgivings, as much as in him lies. The people join in with an 'Amen'. Then takes place the distribution to all those present of the things over which the thanksgiving has been spoken. The deacons bring a portion to those absent. Moreover those who are well-off give whatever they will; what is collected is left with the president, who uses it to help orphans and widows, those in want owing to sickness or any other cause, prisoners, travellers, and in short anyone who is in any need.

Take a reflective twenty minutes in a quiet space to read and allow this extract from St Justin to speak to you.

13 ST JUSTIN'S MASS

Whenever I read this account I sense the hair on the back of my neck stand upright. It is quite extraordinary that if Justin walked in on a celebration of the Eucharist today he might be surprised to discover how little had changed. How right and how wrong he would be.

So many changes took place over nineteen hundred years. What strikes you from the extract itself? It is a celebration of the community, and that is at the heart of any Christian living. And notice how the celebration spills over to those absent for whatever reason and to a commitment to those 'in any need'. This is a celebration of the reign of God.

Today this sense of communal belonging and companionship may not be a top priority for many believers but it is something that can be at the heart of a living faith where we can be nourished profoundly. Reflect on these words of Michael Paul Gallagher SJ:

> Even though you may think of the church with little enthusiasm, or even with deep distrust, ask yourself whether you need to invent the wheel again. In spite of its frightening failures, the church has been a space of nourishment for countless numbers of people through many centuries. It has developed scaffolding for journeys towards possible faith; through reflection on life and on revelation, through skills of interiority, through sacramental celebration, through the witness of self-giving by ordinary people and by saints. Without some such

companionship with believers, the journey
towards faith can simply be too lonely and
without signposts (Gallagher p 150).

*What sense do you have of belonging within the com-
munity of believers? Are you committed to that belonging? How is that expressed?*

14 BASILICA MASS

When the community of Jesus' followers were allowed to 'come out' and publicly profess and practise their religion – when it became the religion of the Roman Empire – its number grew. Gradually they met for the celebration of the Eucharist in large buildings, public areas. With Christianity as the religion of the state many of the civil ceremonial rites and customs were transferred to the liturgy: bowing, incense, elaborate vestments, rings and titles. All this was intended to express reverence for the majesty of God and the liturgy; God deserved the same respect and honour as the Emperor.

Around this time also, theologians were grappling with the reality and complexity of the person of Jesus. Arius in his attempt at understanding concluded that Jesus was fully human but not divine. The reaction to this was that greater and greater emphasis was placed on his divinity and that became the uppermost popular understanding. The corollary of this was a stress on our sinful humanity and our unworthiness. So over time the celebration of the Eucharist lost its intimacy and a gulf arose between what went on 'at the altar' and those present. All the gradual accretions of pomp and ceremony, the imposition of the 'Roman Rite' and the development of complex Gregorian chant gave rise to the people of God at Mass being filled with wonder and awe but with less and less participation and fewer and fewer receiving Holy Communion. Thus the celebration of the Eucharist from around AD 300 to AD 800 became a different experience than in earlier centuries.

How do you express reverence at Mass, interiorly and exteriorly?

15 *MEDIEVAL MASS*

What is referred to as the Medieval Mass covers the years from AD 800 to AD 1500. Controversies arose at this time around the 'Real Presence' and the use of the philosophical concept of 'transubstantiation'. This was an attempt to understand the mystery and the reality of the Eucharistic bread and wine. Stressing the 'Real Presence' further distanced the congregation and fewer again took Holy Communion. As a result greater emphasis was placed on the consecration and the elevation of the Eucharist and less on reception. In fact the Fourth Lateran Council of 1215 made it a church law that we had to receive Holy Communion at least once a year! Had we lived at that time that would have been our practice and understandably so.

It is not intended here to sit in judgement of such developments but only to understand how they came about. No doubt the structuring of society at large over the period had much to do with it too. So it came about that at Mass Christ was to be adored rather than received in communion by 'unworthy' Christians. The expression, 'The gaze that saves' may be very accurate for this period. To avoid crumbs falling, white individual wafers were introduced; they were administered onto the tongues of those, kneeling down at altar rails. At Mass, 'seeing' the host became central and people would attend several Masses to 'see' the host. These expressions of piety gave rise to devotions such as Benediction.

What does 'receiving' Holy Communion mean to you and how does it challenge you?

16 REFORMATION

With the Reformation in full swing the celebration of the Eucharist underwent more developments. Avoiding experimentation, the church imposed a very rigid uniformity on the liturgy. The smallest things became very important and instructions were printed in red, called rubrics. This saved the liturgy from personal innovations and individual exaggerations. However, the continued 'spectator' role of the People of God sat uneasily and extra-liturgical devotions began to appear – such practices as novenas, devotions to the Sacred Heart and Forty Hours Adoration. These were celebrated in the vernacular. The rise of Jansenism,(16th-18th centuries) with its hugely pessimistic theology about people, argued that only those who are 'entirely perfect and perfectly irreproachable' might receive Communion. This had a disastrous effect on the frequency of receiving Holy Communion and led some people to refuse Communion even on their deathbed.

There was a prohibition on translating the Mass books until just before 1900. The beginning of the twentieth century saw developments again. Pope St Pius X promoted the practice of receiving Holy Communion at each Mass. This of course as we know was nothing new. It had fallen out of practice due to historical reasons. Research into earlier liturgical practices, mainly in Benedictine monasteries, opened up a broader understanding of liturgical practices over the centuries. In the mid-twentieth century, the dialogue Mass appeared, with the people reciting parts in Latin. Fasting regulations eased. The Second Vatican Council ushered in many changes so that the people of God could participate more fully in an active, intelligent and easy manner. As the liturgy is a living celebration, changes continue to be made up to the present day. If St Justin visited our Mass today he would sense little had changed, unaware of the changes that have come and gone in the intervening time.

Do you participate in the Eucharist in an active, intelligent and easy manner? How could you improve on this?

Our Sunday Gathering

17 WHAT IDENTITY HAS YOUR GATHERING FOR THE EUCHARIST?

Generally speaking, people like to get together with one another:

> It seems to be a basic human instinct to be relational, to want to share our lives with others and to be part of something bigger than ourselves. We are made for relationships and for community: from our faith community to our family, from neighbourhoods to workplaces, from the global community to the communion of saints.
>
> What has all this to do with what we're about at Sunday Mass? First, although the assembling we do for concerts, rallies or football games is not the same as what we do on Sunday, there are some similarities: 1) as Christians, we identify who we are and believe that this identity is significant; 2) we share certain values to which we can become more deeply committed when we regularly gather together; 3) we can find in the Sunday assembly a sense of unity and support; 4) we celebrate, that is, we remember in a very special way. We remember all that God has done and is doing for us in Jesus Christ and in the power of the Holy Spirit. And unlike other kinds of assemblies, the kind of remembering we do on Sunday is not simply recalling past events, but rather it is a remembering that calls us to attend to God's activity in our lives right now' (Koester, pp 14-15).

How do you react to these similarities and do you have that sense from your Sunday gathering? Finish this sentence in a few ways: 'At Mass I feel ...'

18 THE GATHERING PLACE

As I said earlier the celebration of the Eucharist is a love story; a story of intimacy; an embrace of affirmation, invitation, sacrifice, empathy, compassion, redemption, forgiveness, hope and celebration. The design and architecture of the sacred space should contribute to this sense of intimacy. A sense of everybody belonging within the celebration should dictate the arrangement of the furniture, so to speak. However grandiose and elaborate the space and its furnishings might be, it is essential that a sense of 'them and us' be avoided. All present ought to feel very much included physically if all are to feel 'at home' and participate fully. The focal area for the celebration is called the sanctuary, the place where our story is told and celebrated.

The telling and remembering, the invitation and the challenges of the story take place at the ambo or lectern. This is referred to as the Liturgy of the Word. The Liturgy of the Eucharist/The Breaking of Bread – the celebration of our story – takes place at the altar table. These two elements of the celebration remind us of the two inherent thrusts of our humanity: made in God's image and likeness, to know and to love. The third focal point in the sanctuary during the celebration is the chair for the celebrant who presides over the eucharistic love story. So during the Mass we focus on the ambo, the altar and the celebrant's chair.

The word liturgy, from the Greek language, means the public work of the people. In religious terms it is understood as the participation of the People of God in the work of God, the bringing about of God's reign, God's love story, our love story. We are invited in the liturgy to respond to the unconditional loving approach of God in Christ by orienting the particular story we live towards the example of the life story of Jesus. This is what we ask for in prayer; what we listen to in the silence of our contemplation; what we confront in the highs and lows of everyday life, its joys and pains; what concerns us in the injustices we are aware of in society and church, in the dangers to our environmental well-being. All these experiences are included in our celebration in the sanctuary during the liturgy and in the sanctuary of our daily life where we experience 'God in everything'.

When you go to church where do you sit, and why?

19 *LITURGY AND LIFE: COMPANIONS*

How we conduct the celebration should reflect how we conduct our lives and vice versa. Richard Rohr says that 'how we do anything is how we do everything'. It is one thing to recall and celebrate our love story, it is another thing how we live it all day, every day. The integrity of one reflects the integrity of the other. Jesus said:

> So when you are offering your gift at the altar, if you remember that your brother or sister has something against you, leave your gift there before the altar and go; first be reconciled with your brother or sister, and then come and offer your gift (NRSV, Mt 5: 23-24).

Let us rise to the challenge of this invitation. How we celebrate the liturgy can help us in how we live each day and how we live each day can help us in our celebration of the liturgy. How I hold my sick child may be reflected in how I hold the ciborium. How I am present to my dying father may be reflected in how present I am as I proclaim or hear the word of God at Mass. How I seriously enjoy the company of family and friends may be reflected in how seriously I enjoy the company of those at the Eucharist. How I hear the call to act justly at Mass may be reflected in how I am involved in politics or with justice groups or support them financially. How I hear the call to forgive may be reflected in how I am open to reconciliation. How I understand the sacrifice of the Mass may lead me to a better understanding of 'sacrifice' in my life. How I use the goods of life must reflect how I use the goods of the liturgy. In the *Rule of St Benedict* he writes about the monk in charge of the goods of the monastery: 'He will regard all utensils and goods of the monastery as sacred vessels of the altar.' (*The Rule of St Benedict in English*, Liturgical Press, 1981, p 55). Liturgy and life – mutually challenging and fulfilling!

Reflect on Richard Rohr's words:
'How we do anything is how we do everything.' Is there
an invitation here?

20 *THE FLOW AND RHYTHM OF THE CELEBRATION*

The celebration of the Eucharist may be compared to a party or a drama, several movements with high points and quiet times, a flow and a rhythm. If you are celebrating some occasion – birthday, anniversary, wedding, funeral – invitations go out and people gather on the day, with the theme of the gathering in their minds. They greet one another and begin to talk and listen – to their life stories. Then they celebrate their gathering over food and drink at table. Memories are recalled and lived again in the moment. Finally things wind down with final goodbyes, friendships renewed and promises to keep in touch. Mass follows a similar pattern: the invitation, the moments of gathering and departing – the Introductory and Dismissal Rites – with the storytelling and sharing of food – the Liturgies of the Word and of the Eucharist. We will look at these parts in turn. However:

> In participating in the celebration, it is important to 'go with the flow' of the natural rhythm of the ritual. That rhythm leads to a kind of peak at the gospel, the high point of the proclamation of the Word, then ebbs a bit through the preparation of the gifts. The Eucharistic Prayer is the most central part of the Mass, with the sharing in Communion following as a climactic point flowing from the Eucharistic Prayer. The ritual quickly tapers off to the dismissal, sending us forth renewed and recommitted ... The goal of worship

is the human-divine encounter, and God is always in charge of that. To meet with the Eternal One, we can only open our hearts and prepare ourselves; we cannot make it happen. All too often we march through the liturgy, clergy and laity alike, as if we know exactly what will happen, and the net effect of that attitude is that nothing is likely to happen at all. Our God is a God of surprises, and we had best be prepared to be surprised if we seek a meeting with the Holy One (Mick, p 24).

Consider the similarities mentioned above. Do they make sense? Do you 'march through the liturgy' or are you prepared for surprises? How can you change?

21 INTRODUCTORY RITE

As I have said before going to church is a definite choice and this is reflected in the entrance procession during which we stand in participation. The celebrant kisses the altar as a sign of reverence for Christ, the great lover, the 'firstborn' in our story, through whom 'the love of God is poured into our hearts'. All present 'blessing themselves' with the sign of the cross proclaim who it is that has gathered together and the greeting: 'The Lord be with you' recognises the church as the People of God, the Body of Christ. The penitential rite reminds us of God's great love and compassion and of the fact that we are much loved and already forgiven for the ways we have failed to bring about the reign of God, within us and within the world. This is one reason why we give thanks – Eucharist.

Already we are becoming a praying community, essential to the fruitful celebration of the Eucharist. The celebrant invites us to pray and during the silence we touch in our hearts those people and circumstances we wish to bring to prayer. The priest then recites the Collect, the first solemn prayer of the Mass. It usually refers to the theme of the particular day and we assent to this prayer with our 'Amen'. At this stage we recognise who we are as a sacred community gathered together, leaving aside all our preoccupations for a while and focus on the community with whom we stand, aware of the presence of God in our gathering and the particular theme of the celebration.

'Blessing yourself' … what does this mean to you?

22 *LITURGY: THE WORD*

This part of the Mass is the telling, listening and challenging around our love story. In this liturgy we believe that the Word of God, Jesus the Christ, becomes present in the gathered community as Word. We listen to our story – who we are, where we have come from, where we are called to. It is of course part history, but at the heart of it is the truth that we seek and long for as we muddle our way through life, surrounded by life and death, pain and joy, horror and ecstasy. The first two readings, from the Old and New Testaments are taken by a Minister of the Word, while a cantor may take the psalm. The celebrant or deacon proclaims the gospel. Most of us are actively reading in our missalettes what is being proclaimed from the ambo. Some liturgists suggest that as a living word is being proclaimed we should not read but rather focus on the reader with reverence and care. Ministry of the Word is not to be taken lightly; it is a sacred duty and calls for prayerful preparation and to be carried out with skill and reverence. The people present, by focusing on the reader and the proclamation, will in turn empower the reader to perform the ministry with care and reverence. Eye contact is recommended during the reading. If I am proclaiming a living word to God's people, I ought to look at them. In this way God's word will find a fruitful heart to land in.

We stand as a mark of honour for the reading of the gospel. All are invited to sign the cross on their forehead, lips and heart. We tend to do such signs in haste and may lose their meaning and significance. These three signs of the cross at this point in the Mass have a particular significance. In doing them we pray that the words and values of the gospel may influence us as we strive to embody the reign of God in our lives: forehead – may our thoughts, understanding, discernments and decisions be in tune with the reign of God among us; lips – may what I speak be spoken from the standpoint of one living joyfully in the reign of God; heart – may the words of the gospel influence all I desire, long for and hold dear. So these three intimate signs of the cross remind me of the commitment I have, and long for, to the values of the gospel – values which are found in every human heart as a spark of the divine. They present an invitation to respond to the challenge of God who meets us in the bits and pieces of everyday life.

After the proclamation of the gospel it might be good if the celebrant invited us to be silent for some minutes to allow the words to settle in our hearts. The celebrant now gives the homily, where the word is broken open for us, applying it to our lives today, here and now.

Would you consider reading the passages from scripture for the following Sunday during the week and reflecting on them over the week?
See www.tarsus.ie and click on The Sunday Gospels for the readings and reflections. Or google Sunday Readings Catholic Church for other options.

23 COMMITMENT

We are now invited to stand and pray the creed. It is placed here as a preparation for the Liturgy of the Eucharist. Those who stand around the table of the Eucharist are those who have been baptised and share in the teachings of the community. As St Justin said: 'No one may partake of the Eucharist unless he is convinced of the truth of our teachings and is cleansed in the bath of baptism.' It was at this point in the liturgy that those preparing for baptism used to leave, sent out by the community of the faithful, knowing that when their time of preparation for baptism was completed they would be welcomed fully into the community and fully celebrate the Eucharist. The Mass to this point was once called the Mass of the Catechumens.

The Prayers of the Faithful follow, so called as those remaining after the dismissal of the catechumens were the 'faithful'. The prayers of intercession are very inclusive – for the Christian community, the civil authorities and the needs of the world, those who are excluded and oppressed and for local needs. This too is part of our love story – expressing our concern for all people and living out that concern. The intention raised in our prayer is not to shift responsibility to God but to call to mind our responsibility to love – near and far – and to be available to involve ourselves in the work of God, the bringing about of God's reign.

This brings to an end the Liturgy of the Word, where we listen, learn, pray, are challenged, sit in silence, all around the Word of God, the proclamation of which is intended to spur us to be the unconditional love, the compassion and loving kindness of God in the world.

Do you share the teachings of the community? How do you express these?

24 LITURGY OF THE EUCHARIST: PREPARATIONS

We now begin the second part of our celebration, focusing on 'the breaking of bread'. This part also has its moments of highs and lows. The table of the Eucharist is now prepared, followed by the Eucharistic Prayer and then Holy Communion.

The altar table should be utterly simple and uncluttered. A white cloth covers the entire surface and a smaller one, the corporal, at the centre. On this are placed the chalice, the paten, and the ciboria. Candles are also placed on the table and the altar missal. For Benediction and the Exposition of the Blessed Sacrament the monstrance is used and for those taking Holy Communion to the sick and housebound a small container, the pyx, is used. The bread is simple unleavened bread – made mostly by enclosed orders of nuns.

It is customary at this time to have a collection for the support of the clergy and the church. As we saw this custom was well established by the time of St Justin though the gifts were more than just money:

> This is the point in the Mass when the collection is taken up – at the moment the bread and wine are being placed on the table. Why? For many centuries it was not only bread and wine which were brought up. People brought up corn and oil and eggs and cheese and spare clothing – whatever they had that they didn't need for themselves. It was the moment of redistributing the wealth of the community ... They could not celebrate the

memory of Jesus' gift of himself without themselves being generous with one another ... To remember Christ was not just to think about him: it was to live as he lived and to love as he loved, in very practical ways (Searle 58).

How do you 'remember' Christ in practical ways?

25 THINGS SACRED

This is a rather busy part of the Eucharist: collection, gifts being brought forward and setting the table. It is nonetheless part of the flow of the Mass and should be carried out with great reverence and dignity. As mentioned before how we do anything is how we do everything. Searle is very clear and challenging about all the elements of the Mass and their place in our celebration and in our life:

> Liturgy is not so much a celebration of life-as-we-know-it as it is a celebration of the mystery of life we hardly suspect. While it uses the stuff of everyday life – word and song, movement and food, meeting and touching, candles and flowers, tables and chairs – it uses them all with a sense of the holiness of these things. This holiness is derived not so much from their presence in a sacred place as from a recognition of the sacred presence which pervades all places. The people and language and things of the liturgy are to be handled with reverence and care. Ours is a pragmatic culture, with little sense of the lovely. Part of our liturgical ministry will be to ensure that the things we use and the things we do liturgically serve to develop people's sensitivity to the loveliness of all created things, a loveliness which is but an expression and reflection of the Creator himself (Searle pp 30-31).

How do you behave around 'the sacred presence which pervades all places … the loveliness of all created things'? Remember: 'The fullness of joy is to behold God in everything!'

26 FRUIT OF THE EARTH AND WORK OF HUMAN HANDS

The celebrant prays using sentiments from the ancient Jewish Beracha tradition: 'Blessed are you Lord God of all creation. Through your goodness we have this bread/wine to offer.' We are reminded that the bread and wine are gifts of God, fruits of the earth and work of human hands. Once again Searle speaks very aptly:

> The mere putting of bread and wine on the table became significant. Even today, men or women will talk of their struggle to put bread on the table. But here is no ordinary table. It is the table prepared by God for his people in the person of his Son. As such it becomes a paradigm for all tables everywhere, making us recognise in all food and drink the fruit of the earth and the work of human hands: the gift of God and his human co-workers. It makes us see that all human labour is a co-operative venture. We dig and plant, but God gives the growth. We transform the world by our technology, but God gives the raw materials and the skill (Searle p 58).

What is in your mind as you buy and put 'food on the table'?

27 *EUCHARISTIC PRAYER*

The Eucharistic Prayer begins with a dialogue and the Preface and ends with the great Amen, again customary in St Justin's time. There follows a choice of Eucharistic Prayer, all following a pattern. At its heart, the consecration is about the self-giving life and death of Christ; his sacrifice, resurrection and ascension. This self-giving resides in the self-giving of the Father, and it is the invitation extended to us.

The words of the institution are taken from sacred scripture and have been used throughout the two millennia of Christianity. One paraphrase might be: 'Do this in order to bring about my presence, to make really present the salvation wrought in me.' The story of this salvation, God's unconditional loving and indiscriminate welcoming – our love story – is lived out continuously, flowing from the celebration of the Eucharist into life and from life back into the Eucharist. At the end of the Eucharistic Prayer we are called on to give our consent and we do this with what is called the 'Great Amen'. The Hebrew word 'Amen' has associations with the idea of pounding one's tent stakes in the ground. How you pound in that stake will determine how secure your tent is. So by saying your 'Amen' you are saying in a way 'I am staking my life on it.'

Your lifestyle is chosen around the self-giving lifestyle of Jesus. Once again at Mass we are reminded of the three signs of the cross at the gospel: the invitation to live truly the reign of God, a reign of truth and justice, of love and peace.

Next time you say the great 'Amen' ... mean it and follow through!

28 THE COMMUNION RITE

This begins with the great Christian prayer, the Our Father. What a wealth of meaning is found in those first two words of the prayer that Jesus gave us. It sums up all his life – a life lived in union with the love and compassion, the welcome and forgiveness of his Abba, his Father. This is the challenge for us, to live in that same mode. It is very fitting to have this prayer as the opening of the Communion Rite. We pray for our 'daily bread', bread that comes from God, symbolised in the Eucharist. Part of this bread and prayer also is the forgiveness that the sacrifice of Christ extends to us, and which we commit to extend to others.

This challenge is made obvious in the exchange of peace that follows. When we say: 'The peace of Christ be with you' we are in a way committing ourselves to reconciliation in all its dimensions, prior to accepting Holy Communion. Otherwise we lose the meaning of what is involved. When Jesus said: 'Do this ...' it is an invitation to live a eucharistic lifestyle, not just a moment on a Sunday.

Be deliberate when you exchange the sign of peace at the Eucharist ... and to the challenge it presents.

29 *THE BREAKING OF BREAD*

The early Christians referred to the Eucharist as 'the breaking of bread'. What a significant description! Is that what you do when you share a meal, break bread together? Families, friends and colleagues do this. What does it mean, if anything? In modern families, do the members eat together? Are meals together more than 'feeding time'? Once again remind yourself that the Eucharist revolves around a love story ... can sharing meals with friends/ family do likewise? Sharing meals is very much an expression of love and closeness. Perhaps here you might stop reading and reflect a little ... taking a moment of reflection is like allowing our hearts to recognise what is all around us and relishing the moment, the power of 'now'.

At the last supper Jesus broke the bread and passed it around. This gesture has become very much a cornerstone of what the Eucharist means. St Paul says: 'Because there is one bread, we who are many are one body, for we all partake of the one bread' (1Cor 10:17).

> This one body signifies a unity which triumphs over all human differences, prejudices and inequalities. A sacrament is not just an empty sign, an aesthetic symbol: it contains and requires what it signifies. The breaking of bread is a sacramental sign of the irrelevance of our divisions and classes. It makes them irrelevant. But we have to take that seriously in our own lives, which means living as if there were no classes, no racial differences, no social or economic barriers between people. It means dropping our grudges and our suspicions

and our prejudices. For this reason, the actual breaking of bread is preceded by the Our Father and the exchange of peace (Searle pp 67-68).

Take some time to reflect on how you 'break bread' with others – your family, relations, those poorer than you, those you dislike, those seriously 'different' from you. Does 'breaking bread' at the Eucharist colour your attitudes and your behaviour?

Time to minister

30 MINISTERING HOLY COMMUNION

This is where you respond to the invitation to be a minister of the Eucharist. All the discernment, preparation, reflection time and prayer now bear down on your ministry. Are you up to it? Do you take the ministry seriously and desire to perform it with reverence and care?

It is essential that your ministry be personal; you are not a vending machine. Once again remember Richard Rohr: 'How we do anything is how we do everything.' How you are with people generally will be reflected in how you are with those you minister to. You are not asked to be 'different' for the moments you spend ministering Holy Communion. The reverence, care and ease you show during communion time should reflect how you are at other times. Take a few moments to consider this seriously. If you put on a 'mask' for your ministry ... what does that mean? This is a moment of discovering perhaps how you are with people generally; being a Eucharistic Minister can challenge and teach us about ourselves. When a person stands in front of you for Communion you are challenged not to consider their status, beauty, sex, sexual orientation, age, disability or race. You have just prayed 'Our Father'! You are called on to be as person-centred as Jesus was, to extend a gracious welcome to all, indiscriminately, and to mirror his

inclusive table companionship. As regards disabili-
ties you should allow the person to decide how they
wish to receive Holy Communion, in their seat or
by coming forward with others.

How are you with people, in life, in family,
in work, in church?
What 'masks' might interfere with your ministry?

31 THE MORNING AFTER THE NIGHT BEFORE

It may arise in your ministry that you feel on a particular day that you are not able/ready/worthy to minister Holy Communion. This may be because of something you did the previous day/week and you are not in a good space because of it. This is bound to happen and it happens also to the clergy and even to bishops. God does not call you to ministry because you are worthy. That may be one of the surprises you come to recognise. In a situation like this you may need a little quiet time to reflect. Listen and respond to the words of Psalm 15:

> O Beloved, you invite us to rest in the abode of your heart, to forgive our weaknesses and renew our love? Who will respond with hearts opened wide to love ... Those whose weaknesses are acknowledged and brought to light in prayer' (Merrill, p 19).

You are needed for the ministry on a particular day and if needs be you might choose to avail of the sacrament of Reconciliation later. Remember integrity and purity of heart. You might find the following thoughts helpful:

> Chastity has to do with all experiencing. It is about the appropriateness of any experience. Ultimately chastity is reverence – and sin, all sin is irreverence. To be chaste is to experience people, things, places, entertainment, the phases of our lives, and sex in a way that does not violate them or ourselves. To be chaste is to experience things reverently, in such a way that the experience leaves both them and ourselves more, not less, integrated. Thus we are

chaste when we relate to others in a way that does not transgress their moral, psychological, emotional, aesthetic, and sexual boundaries. That is an abstract way of saying that we are chaste when we do not let impatience, irreverence, or selfishness ruin what is gift by somehow violating it. Conversely, we lack chastity when we cross boundaries prematurely or irreverently, when we violate anything and somehow reduce what it is. Chastity is respect, reverence, and patience. Its fruits are integration, gratitude and joy. Lack of chastity is impatience, irreverence, and violation. Its fruits are disintegration of soul, bitterness, and cynicism (Rolheiser, p 191).

Sometimes you may have second thoughts about ministering on a particular day ... it might be wise preparing for such occasions in advance, using the thoughts above.

32 *SPEEDY?*

I can remember in my youth when the priest was ministering Holy Communion there would be long lines at the altar rails and he would move along speedily, saying the long Latin prayer over several communicants, which was meant to be prayed at each individual. With the advent of Eucharistic Ministers the distribution of Holy Communion could happen more slowly and more reverently. The moment of receiving Holy Communion is only that, a moment, but lots can happen in a moment and lots can be missed. You are in charge. The time before you minister is important, time to allow your inner dignity and reverence to come to the fore, time to relax yourself so that your ministry can relax those in your queue. You can create the conditions necessary for the moment to bear fruit. You are part of the communicant's immediate preparation for Communion. She/he deserves your full attention, not to see you checking out your queue, or looking around. Reflect on how Jesus met people in his lifetime: no matter what condition he met them in, all were welcomed with loving-kindness and compassion. The moment of Communion gives you an opportunity to act likewise. Christ is present in the Eucharist but also in you and in the communicant!

Your faith is expressed when you say: 'The Body of Christ' and you call forth the faith of those you serve as they say 'Amen'. In fact their 'Amen' can have a salutary effect on you. This moment can change the way you spend other moments with people, at home, at work, in the supermarket, on the phone. It is important,

> to remember that in the reception of the Eucharist we are not receiving a divine thing or object, we are encountering a person, the risen Christ. The question to ask regarding the Eucharist is not: 'What are we receiving?' but 'Who are we encountering?' Catholics have long turned the word communion into an object as in the phrase 'receiving Holy Communion,' when it originally referred to a relationship, as in the statement: 'We are being drawn into communion with Christ (Gaillardetz, p 22).

Be present to all that is going on within you during these moments of ministering Holy Communion, and take time later to reflect on that. It could be that a moment of grace is being offered and you need to stop and allow it time and space to bear fruit.

33 OCULAR, VERBAL AND TACTILE CONTACT

There are three kinds of necessary contact in the sharing of Holy Communion: ocular, verbal and tactile. Dare to let your eyes meet those of the communicant and reflect the wonder of God's love in the Eucharist. Dare to let your voice announce God's invitation to the banquet of eternal life. Dare to let your hands touch those of the communicant as they minister God's holy gifts. Dare to let the communicant feel the texture of the bread and of your own hand; dare to feel the communicant's own hand (it may be as rough or smooth as your own). It would be possible to place the bread in a person's hand in a more 'antiseptic' way but at the loss of so much of the human, personal warmth of the moment (Kwatera, p 14).

Consider time out in prayer to allow these thoughts to percolate into your mind and heart ... how they might enrich your ministry.

34 THE RITUAL ITSELF

Rituals have several elements: word, gesture and object. I may wish to give flowers to someone I love and these three elements play a part: the words I use, the facial and other expressions I show and, of course, the flowers. If any one element is weak then the ritual loses something of its significance and benefit. The same is true of the ritual of ministering Holy Communion. It needs full attention, concentration and reverence. You should be somewhat tired after distributing Communion if you do it properly.

You ought to be your own regulator. Routine could be disastrous. Do you simple repeat the words in a sing-a-long fashion? Do you wait reverently to hear the communicant's 'Amen' response? Do you become judgemental about how the communicant receives? Do you get shifty when you realise you have a long queue compared to others? Time perhaps to stop and recognise that you may be giving the person in front of you a poor ministry? One antidote is to try to imagine that you are giving Holy Communion to only one person, and that one person is right there in front of you and do not allow any other consideration to impinge on that most sacred of moments. All this may cause a strain on your vocal cords and back. Standing in a comfortable and balanced position is important, feet a little apart, relaxed but fully present. 'Your demeanour should be that of a caring host or hostess, not that of a soldier presenting colours at a graveside' (Kwatera 18).

Take time out after your ministry to observe how you carry out your ministry and be critical and constructive.

35 REVERENCE

This is crucial and is not something you put on, pretend or fake. You can nurture and nourish a reverent attitude to all of life and all you do, say and think as you go about your daily living; in that way it becomes part of who you are! This is the living out of your humanity, your Baptism, your response to the invitation to live the reign of God, where you grow in unconditional love and compassion. If you begin to make this a habit then you will find that reverence during your Communion ministry comes easily and naturally. There is no 'disconnect' with all of life and your ministry. Your reverence during Communion will encourage your reverence generally and vice versa and be a witness to others. Their reverence can be a wake up call for you! This reverence will be observed in how you walk, bow, your demeanour in the sanctuary, your rinsing of fingers (if that is the practice), how you receive Communion yourself, how you pick up, carry and hold the ciborium or chalice, how you return them. All ought to be done carefully and deliberately. Please do not let this reverence show itself by putting on a 'holy' show! Rather let it be natural and warm, with dignity and a gentle smile as you minister with joy and delight, remembering how Jesus was with those he met in his life.

Is reverence something you nourish in your life and ministry? Pray around this.

36 BLESS YOURSELF

What a strange expression! Bless yourself. Yet as a child I remember being encouraged to 'bless myself' with holy water as I left the house. The holy water font hung next to the hall door.

Yet I was given to believe also that only ordained priests could bless. I have grown to believe that we are all called to bless, to call God's blessing on people, events, meals, journeys and crucial moments in life. In some ways this is bringing to mind the fact that these are already blessed and our blessings are spoken in acknowledgment and gratefulness and renew the challenge to be that blessing.

It is customary in some places to offer a blessing to young children and non-communicants who approach you during your ministry. It is like expressing a word of encouragement.

> These blessings may take the form of a small sign of the cross on the forehead, a larger one over the person, or a hand laid on the person's head, with or without words. An extraordinary minister can give such a blessing just as clergy do. But this practice is not required, and it is extraneous to the purpose of the Communion procession: coming forward to receive the Body and Blood of Christ. Also, such blessings are redundant since everyone in the assembly shares in the priest's blessing at the end of Mass (Kwatera 8).

This may be somewhat novel and needs to be addressed. It might be addressed as people prepare for the ministry along with other concerns.

The questions of proper seating, proper dress, and distinctive signs of ministry, and the washing of hands before and after giving Communion, should be answered by the group of ministers themselves in consultation with the liturgy committee and the pastor; they should not be answered by decree of the pastor (Kwatera p 8).

So today, as you leave your home deliberately bless yourself in a 'now' moment, rooted in the depth of your own reality, dignity and integrity – to bless yourself for your leaving and your safe return and that you may be a blessing and a joy/compassion to all you do and all whom you meet today.

37 *THE MASS IS ENDED, GO IN PEACE TO LOVE AND SERVE THE LORD*

What a challenge! Perhaps just before this dismissal there were announcements and some of these may have been suggestions as to how 'to love and serve the Lord'. However the words remind us of our commitment to building the reign of God, our love story. The manner in which the parish liturgy is prepared and celebrated speaks to us of that reign. And we bring to our celebration our work for that reign. Pope John Paul II wrote:

> We mustn't deceive ourselves: it's from our reciprocal love and, in particular, for the concern we have for those in need that we will be recognised as true disciples of Christ. This is the criterion on the basis of which the authenticity of our Eucharistic celebrations will be confirmed (*National Catholic Reporter* on-line October 15, 2004).

How is this reign brought about, this authenticity?

> Wherever the human heart is healed, justice gains a foothold, peace holds sway, an ecological habitat is protected, wherever liberation, hope and healing break through, wherever an act of simple kindness is done, a cup of cool water given, a book offered to a child thirsty for learning, there the human and earth community already reflect, in fragments, the visage of the Trinitarian God. Borne by 'the grace of our Lord Jesus Christ, the love of God, and the fellowship of the Holy Spirit', we become committed to a fruitful future inclusive of all peoples, tribes, and nations, all creatures of the earth. The reign of God gains another foothold in history (Johnson 224).

So you leave your celebration with a challenge. How do you respond to that challenge 'to love and serve the Lord'?

Parting Thoughts

38 YOUR PARISH EUCHARIST

For most of the congregation the Sunday Eucharist is the only contact they have with the Christian community at prayer. It is a time of prayer, praise and learning, moments of grace and surprise, challenge, support and care. Much of this little book concerns the celebration of the Eucharist actively and intelligently, reverently and deliberately. Below is a checklist that might prove helpful in examining how your parish Eucharist is celebrated:

- Is the Sunday Mass a celebration of the entire parochial community, including all movements and sub-groups?
- Is the proclamation of the Word of God, and especially the homily, truly effective in opening up the scriptures? (The pope makes a special point of calling for care in the preparation and delivery of homilies)
- Are the tones of voice, the gestures, the movements, the sense of respect, the moments of silence, and the whole constellation of modes of acting consistent with the dignity of the Eucharist?
- Are people being educated in prayer, especially in the Liturgy of the Hours?
- Are communities engaging in genuine Christian witness outside the liturgy, acting upon the commission at the end of Mass? (Marini)

Reflect on how well your parish performs with this checklist and how can you help?

39 WHAT IS MINISTRY?

Are we 'receivers' of the church's ministry or are we also ministers? Is the church there to dispense grace,

> as, in Jesuit theologian Karl Rahner's phrase, 'a spiritual supermarket' in which each one does his or her own private, personal spiritual shopping, quite regardless of others around? The truth is that, in belonging to the church, we are part of a service orientated community and a community of people who are themselves committed to service – a community which is committed to performing a service in the area in which it exists (Lyons, p 32).

This is the call to follow the life and example of Jesus. The Dominican theologian, Edward Schillebeeckx, re-casting the traditional definition of sacraments as 'an outward sign instituted by Christ to give grace' in personal terms, emphasised that Jesus himself is the primary sacrament in whom God's gracious love became visible, tangible, historical and irrevocable. Our mission as church, as the body of Christ in the world, is to make visible that invisible love of God.

The reign of God we pray for is realised in part by our efforts to respond to that love of God, in seeking new reconciled and redeemed relationships with God and with one another. This involves working from the inside out; ministry must be an expression of the relationship with Jesus and his mission, about 'being' and 'doing'.

Viewed in this perspective, ministry appears to have two essential dimensions, relational and functional. In understanding them, we appreciate more fully the meaning of ministry and ministerial identity. Ministry involves activity. Usually a person does something for someone. The activity may be explicitly religious – prayer, liturgy, preaching. Or it may be less explicitly religious yet grounded in faith and signifying hope in the coming of the kingdom of God-feeding the hungry, giving shelter to the homeless, working for justice, reconciliation and peace. Activity or function does not exhaust the meaning of ministry. Ministerial activity is ultimately directed towards establishing a life in communion with God and with one another, a way of life which manifests the kingdom of God in our midst (Bernardin, p 22).

Do you see yourself as a sacrament in which God's gracious love becomes visible? Does your eucharistic ministry reflect this, and your life?

40 MINISTERING AS CHRIST MINISTERED

Deviant Behaviour.

Jesus behaved in strange and provocative ways.
He constantly flouted the prevailing codes of conduct in the society. He did not observe the accepted norms of ritual purity. He did not care about
the rite of hand-washing before meals. He did not
engage in fasting. He sometimes violated the pre-
scribed norms of sabbath practice. He surrounded
himself with undesirable people, like tax collectors and prostitutes. He was seen in the company
of beggars, hungry people, and the socially marginalised. More specifically, he fraternised and ate
with 'sinners and tax collectors'. He socialised
with women in ways inappropriate to that culture,
and accepted them among his disciples. Mary
Magdalene had an especially important role in
Jesus' movement. He apparently had an unusual-
ly welcoming attitude toward children. There was
nothing haphazard about the way Jesus did these
things. He was intentionally, graphically showing
people that God's reign is open to everyone, with
no one excluded or marginalised (Pagola, p 460).

*Reflect on this statement. How can you show
intentionally and graphically that God's reign is open to
everyone, both in your ministry and in your living?*

41 *A MEDITATION ON THE EUCHARIST*

He was old, tired and sweaty,
pushing his homemade cart down the
alley,
stooping now and then to poke around in
someone's garbage.
I wanted to tell him about Eucharist,
but the look in his eyes,
the despair in his face,
the hopelessness of somebody else's life in
his cart,
told me to forget it.
So I smiled, said: 'Hi!'
and gave him Eucharist.

She was cute, nice build,
too much paint,
a little wobbly on her feet
as she slid from her bar stool,
and very definitely on the make.
'No thanks, not tonight'
and I gave her Eucharist.

She lived alone,
her husband dead,
her family gone.
And she talked at you, not to you,
words, endless words, spewed out.
So I listened
And gave her Eucharist.

Downtown is nice,
lights change from red to green
and back again.
Flashing blues, pinks, and oranges.

I gulped them in,
said: 'Thank you, Father.'
And made them Eucharist.

I laughed at myself,
and told myself,
'You with all your sin,
and your selfishness,
I forgive you,
I accept you,
I love you.'
It's nice and so necessary too
to give yourself Eucharist.

Tired, weary, disgusted, lonely,
go to your friends,
open your door,
Say: 'Look at me'
and receive their Eucharist.

My Father, when will we learn
you cannot talk Eucharist,
cannot philosophise about it,
you do it.

You don't dogmatise Eucharist,
sometimes you laugh it,
sometimes you cry it,
often you sing it.
Sometimes it is wild peace,
then crying hurt,
often humiliating,
never deserved.

You see Eucharist in another's eyes,
give it in a hand held tight,
squeeze it with an embrace.

You pause Eucharist in the middle of a
busy day,
live Eucharist with a million things to do
and a person who wants to talk.
For Eucharist is as simple as being on time
and as profound as sympathy.

I give you my supper.
I give you my sustenance.
I give you my life.
I give you me.
I give to you...
Eucharist.

Author Unknown

Bibliography

Bernardin, Joseph Cardinal, *The Ministry of Service*, The Liturgical Press, 1985

Cantalamessa, Raniero, *The Eucharist, Our Sanctification*, The Liturgical Press, 1993

Communion, New Parish Ministries, Novalis/Collins, 1987

Gaillardetz, Richard R., *Broken & Poured Out, A Spirituality for Eucharistic Ministers*, Liguori Publications, 2002

Gallagher, Michael Paul, *Faith Maps*, Darton, Longman and Todd, 2010

Johnson, Elizabeth A., *Quest for the Living God*, Continuum, 2008

Koester, Anne Y., *Sunday Mass, Our Role and Why It Matters* Liturgical Press, 2007

Kwatera OSB, Mark, *The Ministry of Communion*, The Liturgical Press, 2004

Lyons, Enda, *Partnership in Parish*, Columba Press, 1987

Marini, Archbishop Piero (the pope's chief liturgist), *National Catholic Reporter* on-line, October 15, 2004, reporting a press conference

Merrill, Nan C., *Psalms for Praying, An Invitation to Wholeness*, Continuum, 2007

Mick, Lawrence E., *Understanding The Sacraments: Eucharist*, The Liturgical Press, 2007

Pagola, Jose, *Jesus, An Historical Approximation*, Convivium Press, 2009

Rolheiser, Ronald, *Seeking Spirituality*, Hodder & Stoughton, 1998

Searle, Mark, *Liturgy Made Simple*, The Liturgical Press, 1981